Successful
Customer
Care

John Wellemin

BARRON'S

All inquiries should be addressed to:
Barron's Educational Series, Inc.
250 Wireless Boulevard
Hauppauge, New York 11788

Library of Congress Catalog Card No. 96-46466

International Standard Book No. 0-7641-0127-7

Library of Congress Cataloging-in-Publication Data
Wellemin, John H..
    Successful customer care / John Wellemin.
       p.   cm. — (Barron's business success series)
    Includes index.
    ISBN 0-7641-0127-7
    1. Customer services. I. Title. II. Series
HF5415.5.W38 1997
658.8'12—dc20   96-46466
                                                      CIP

PRINTED IN HONG KONG
987654321

Contents

Introduction

◆

Why do we need a book about customer care? After all, top management in many companies have always been telling everyone, and particularly their customers and staff, that customer satisfaction is the company's prime aim.

In many instances that was all that top management did about it—talk. More and more companies now realize that positive action is required to ensure that words do not remain mere platitudes. Often, management actions and attitudes contradict the stated intent to regard customer satisfaction as their highest priority.

The implementation of this book's customer care recommendations—although targeted to first-line management—requires focused, continuous, and participative attention from top decision-making management in order to experience the full benefits of these recommendations. In order to achieve this trick (believe me, it's not always easy) communication between first-line management and top management must be nothing short of excellent. This can be achieved by first-line management requesting that top managers read this book or the portions of the book that have been marked for top management attention (to shorten the reading involved). It can also be achieved by first-line management making recommendations, based on the information gained from the book, to top management. This is not an easy path either, because top management egos and "not my idea" are frequently major hurdles to overcome.

Successful and broad communication throughout the company is a bottom line requirement for successful customer care.

After reading this book you will better understand:

- ◆ What customer care is and its effect on profits

- ◆ The role of the first-line manager in customer care

- ◆ The role of top management in customer care

- ◆ The meaning of customer care and its use as a competitive tool

- ◆ The elements influencing customer care

- ◆ Ways of enhancing customer relations

- ◆ The importance of communication

- ◆ How to turn a complaint into a positive experience

- ◆ Why involvement of all staff is essential

- ◆ The need for setting standards and monitoring results

- ◆ Some management tools and aids available

- ◆ How to develop and implement a customer care program

- ◆ Ways of building on past successes

Chapter 1

Customer Care
in General

This chapter will deepen your understanding of:

◆ What customer care is

◆ The value added by customer care

◆ The reason for its growing importance

◆ The role of the first-line manager

The quality of the product or service (for brevity's sake, please assume it means *product or service* when you see *product* in the rest of this book) is a prerequisite for fighting the competitive battle in the marketplace. Customers are entitled to presume that the product they intend to purchase is high quality, and they will make their purchasing decisions based on a much wider range of requirements. The companies that will be able to satisfy the largest number of these needs will be the winners in the long term.

We will examine a little later how you can establish what customers really expect from you as suppliers of their needs. What you must be convinced of is that satisfying these needs as fully as possible will make your products more desirable in the eyes of the customer, make him pay a premium for this benefit, and this in turn will improve your long-term success.

This customer care (or support) adds to the perceived value of your product and will encourage customers to come back to your company when they need to replace it or when they need another product in your range.

Tom Peters put it extremely succinctly when he wrote, "The essence of excellence is the thousand concrete, minute actions performed by everyone in an organization to keep a company on course." (*In Search of Excellence*, T. J. Peters and R. H. Waterman. Harper and Row, 1982).

WHAT IS CUSTOMER CARE?

Before we examine this question let us identify the purpose of a business. The immediate conclusion will be that profit must be the aim of all companies, because without profit, a business cannot survive in the long term. We need to look into this simple statement more deeply.

What enables a company to make a profit? First, it needs to satisfy customer needs at a price the customer is willing and able to pay. Second, the supplier must be able to make or procure the product or service at a cost that, after adding overhead, still falls sufficiently below the price that can be charged to customers to allow a reasonable profit margin. Thus a company can work on:

♦ making the total product offered to the customer more attractive

♦ reducing the cost of the product and/or of the company's overhead

♦ reducing its profit margin per unit of product

Obviously, the best option is to make the total product offering as attractive as possible to the customer to warrant charging a higher price. This, of course, does not preclude working as efficiently as possible to reduce costs or considering lower margins on a unit basis to attract more sales. These latter options tend to be more difficult to accomplish and may also have adverse effects on shareholder satisfaction respectively.

Although these facts have been recognized, many companies concentrate exclusively on the features, quality, and availability of their products. As long as the product is genuinely unique, the customer may have little choice but to purchase from the supplier. An example of this would be the situation that IBM and IBM PC clone computer manufacturers were faced with in the mid to late 1980s. At the time, Intel was the only manufacturer producing an appropriate processing chip that would allow these computers to process DOS based software. Later around 1990, other chip manufacturers began producing chips to the upgraded IBM PC standard (386, 486, Pentium, etc.), creating competition for Intel. In most cases, products are not unique or do not, as in the case of Intel, remain unique forever.

Value to the customer can be added by nonproduct activities. These activities can take many forms. For instance, more helpful counter clerks at an airline check-in counter, improved layout and sign posting in a supermarket, a more customer-orientated waiting line system in a bank or post office, easier telephone access to individual departments, more thoughtful parking arrangements for customers, etc. If we really give this matter some thought, all of us can think of our specific likes and dislikes and find ways of improving how we, as customers, are dealt with.

Think about your company's working procedures. Examine customer requirements and preferences very carefully and introduce necessary changes in your procedures and activities.

Now let us come back to "What is customer care?" It consists of a variety of tangible and intangible elements.

Tangible elements
Tangible factors can be seen or felt, heard or tasted. Many of these factors can be measured relatively easily. They are often based on skills that can be taught and learned. Examples of tangible elements include aspects such as product features (e.g., size, weight, color, speed, ease of access, etc.).

Intangible elements
Intangible elements are much more difficult to define. They are also more difficult to measure and are often more subjective. They are

highly dependent on attitudes that can be influenced but not taught. Examples of intangible elements include making the customer feel secure, relaxed, trusting, and well disposed towards the supplier and the individual staff members.

Because customer care consists of both these elements, it is the responsibility of a manager to ensure that:

◆ The relevant skills are available by either recruiting staff who have already acquired these skills or by ensuring that these skills are imparted to existing or new staff by training, example, and leadership.

◆ The right environment exists or is created to influence the attitude of your staff and, through the employees' attitude, to ensure that the customer is positively disposed towards the company and its employees.

It is much easier for a competitor to copy features of a product, imitate a service or utilize improved tools and equipment than it is to improve on the intangible elements; it is a much longer process that needs to be sustained continuously.

If customers believe you really *care* about resolving their issues, they will come back and remain loyal customers. In this context, remember the long-established fact that it costs about five times as much to acquire a new customer than it does to keep an existing one.

An example of tangible and intangible elements is in the highly competitive automotive industry. The Saturn Corporation, a division of General Motors, decided to do business in a way that emphasized customer care in both tangible and intangible elements as had never been tried in the American automotive business before. At the beginning of the design and manufacture of the Saturn automobile Saturn introduced total quality management and continuous improvement systems and a management organization modeled after the most successful and efficient Japanese automaker management organizations. The result was an automobile whose quality and reliability matched and in some ways exceeded even the high standards set by the Japanese auto manufacturers. Saturn also embarked on a program of customer before sales and after sales satisfaction.

All sales pressure was taken out of the showroom, sticker prices were fixed at very competitive levels, no dickering or negotiating was allowed. If the customer felt the car was too expensive, she left on the best of terms to buy her car elsewhere. When a major defect (there were few) was encountered with the early models, Saturn took the Nordstrom approach, they replaced the entire vehicle with a new one, without a demur and at no cost to the customer. The replacement car was driven to the customer's home, where the exchange took place with a minimum of fuss.

After sales, maintenance and warranty work was conducted with a minimum of disruption to the customer with free loaner cars and rides home. Unsolicited phone calls from Saturn to the customer were made after a few months just to ask if the customer was still satisfied with his car. This approach by Saturn was certainly costly to the company, but in the long run created what are probably the most loyal customers in the industry and repeat sales that go with loyal customers, resulting ultimately in a profitable business. All this with a product that the road testers said was an out-of-date automobile when it was introduced in 1990.

VALUE ADDED BY CUSTOMER CARE

Your customers are usually not looking for the cheapest product with its connotation of low quality. What they are seeking is the best value for the money, which means you need a much broader view of their needs. Some of these requirements may be real, others imagined, but to the individual customer the imagined need may be as important as the real one.

At the same time your product is, in most cases, not unique and the customer will therefore examine a number of suppliers' total offerings to find one that, in the customer's perception, satisfies most of his real or imagined needs. The customer will choose the supplier with whose total package he is most comfortable.

However, you must be able to satisfy these additional customer needs at a cost that the customer is willing to pay and that will be seen by the buyer as sufficient reason to use you or warrant your premium price. Satisfying these additional needs is seen by the customer as adding value to the basic product.

Adding value through customer care is unlikely to add substantially to your costs, and it may well be possible to satisfy your customers' needs at the same or even lower costs. In the following chapters we will discuss how this can be achieved. In some instances there may be a need for some initial expenditure or investment, but it should be possible to recover more than this outlay in the long run. The aim of customer care is to make the customer feel good about doing business with you and to make the customer want your product exclusively.

You must find out what the customer expects from you both in the area of the product and service you are providing and in the broader field of your total offering; only then will customers feel satisfied and be willing to continue to do business with you. All customers want to feel they are important and you must therefore treat them as individuals to show them that they are important. Without customers there would be no need for your company's products or your work.

Adding value through customer care is therefore a question of doing your individual jobs as effectively as possible and keeping the customer's needs in mind when performing your tasks.

Remember, computer customers want to keep computing, not twiddle their thumbs for the two weeks it takes for their defective computer to go back to the factory, get fixed, and returned. Automobile customers want to keep driving, not have to worry about bus schedules, or rides with spouses or friends to drop off their defective car and wait until it's fixed (hours, sometimes days).

Airlines want to keep flying on schedule with a safe aircraft. For that reason, at every major airport in the country there are airframe experts, engine experts, wheel and brake experts, electrical experts, and hydraulic experts constantly diagnosing problems and supplying replacements for worn or defective components—all working to keep their customer, the airline, in profitable business. The end use customer, the passenger, enjoys the convenience and safety that all of this activity provides.

In Chapter 2, we will examine who your customer really is.

THE GROWING IMPORTANCE OF CUSTOMER CARE

Let us first of all list some of the main reasons for the growing influence of customer care in the buyers' purchasing decisions and then we will discuss each one of them in more detail:

◆ Increased competition—the customer has a choice

◆ Better informed customers

◆ Product similarity—need to differentiate suppliers

◆ Rising demand for improved support

◆ Life-cycle cost considerations—maintenance costs play an increasing part

◆ Willingness of customers to pay for real or perceived value

◆ Integration of customers' own work with suppliers' products and services

◆ Desire to concentrate on own mainstream activities

Can you add to this list? Examine your working environment and you will certainly come up with a number of additional reasons.

Let us expand on each of these points, starting with, perhaps, the most important one.

Competition

It is only natural that where there is an attractive market, competitors will seek to obtain profitable business. The newcomer may sometimes even have an advantage due to the fact that he may have benefited from the experience of the long-established supplier. As the newcomers start from scratch, they can use the latest equipment, techniques, and systems and can select staff to fit the image they wish to create. Some of the factories built, for example, by Japanese companies in Europe tend to use more modern manufacturing and management techniques, and these flexible manufacturing, custom-built factories are more efficient than old, established companies.

Competition gives customers greater choice and they will therefore become more selective and knowledgeable about various suppliers.

With the signing of the latest Gatt Trade Agreement, the trend over the last few years has been to make many businesses work on a global basis, which further increases competition, not only from local sources, but also from overseas.

The creation of the European Union and the North American Free Trade Association has made it easier to do business in all countries of the EU and North America. Thus it not only offers an opportunity for companies to expand outside their own countries, but it also opens up local markets to competition from abroad.

You should not look at competition as something negative; it is likely to force your business to become more efficient and is forcing many companies to become more customer orientated. This is a direction they should have taken in any case.

An example of a highly competitive business activity is the airline business. A number of years ago a small airline, Southwest Airlines, decided to depart from the normal way of providing transportation service to the general public and provide them with what Southwest believed to be what these customers really wanted: low fares and a no-fuss safe and efficient airline. Southwest decided that elimination of first and business classes and elimination of in-flight meals and other perks would not deter their low-fare customers.

Southwest's efficiency was enhanced by their exclusive use of one type of aircraft, the Boeing 737, and by speeding up airport check-in and aircraft turnaround between flights.

Southwest, by understanding the customer's true needs, quickly began to dominate most short haul routes in the west and southwest United States, and at the same time became the most profitable airline in the United States. Other airlines have modified their operations, in many cases copying Southwest's methods, in order to compete.

Better informed customers

Customers know a great deal more about your products and support activities than they used to, partly because of the above-mentioned competition and partly due to the extensive studies conducted by consumer groups, consumer magazines, professional associations, and other institutions. The media also tend to discuss in some depth the merits and demerits of various products. The emphasis put into competitive advertisements also makes customers more aware of the aspects they should examine. The financial services industry is a good example, where public pressure has forced regulations on the industry, ensuring fuller disclosure of costs and more realistic estimates of benefits.

Product similarity

From the customer's point of view, it is difficult to distinguish many of your products from those of your competitors. They often use the same components and perform the same tasks in a very similar way. As an example, look at the personal computer industry, where a large number of computers have similar processing chips and can utilize the same software programs. One of the few ways you can differentiate yourselves from your competitors is by means of the image for customer care that you create and the reputation for customer support that you have earned over time.

Rising demand for improved support

With the choice of supply sources now available to your customers they know that they are in a buyers' market and they are therefore demanding improved support from the suppliers they have selected. In general, it has been shown that with a higher living standard, customers are willing (and able) to pay for improved support. For instance, customers in the past may have been willing to wait for a week or two for a telephone to be installed whereas now they expect it to be done in a few days.

Life-cycle costs

As many products are technically more sophisticated, customers have become more dependent on the continuing support from you to keep their products in operation. They are increasingly looking at the lifetime costs and your ability to support their products efficiently throughout the life of that product. When a customer buys a car, for instance, he will want to know how good the warranty is, how good the maintenance service is, what the costs are likely to be, the fuel consumption and the resale value after a certain number of years.

Willingness of customers to pay for value added

Customers are increasingly realizing the cost of their own time and the penalty cost for having to delay actions, negotiate replacements or delivery schedules. In consequence, they are also willing to pay a premium to suppliers who offer them better service, who can accommodate changes at shorter notice and who can be generally relied upon. The Just in Time (JIT) approach discussed in the next section is a typical example.

Integration of customers' own work with suppliers' products

As customers have come under greater pressure to cut costs, they have become aware of the need to integrate operations with those of their suppliers to simplify the work process. Let us examine two of these areas.

First, there has been a move towards suppliers delivering goods just in time (JIT) when they are needed by the customer. This has advantages for the customer, who does not need to hold large buffer stocks (less stock holding, no double handling, less obsolescence, less space requirement), but it puts pressure on the suppliers. They have to become more flexible in providing products when needed, the agreed quality has to be met all the time (rejects would immediately affect the customer's schedule), and delivery dates have to be strictly adhered to. For this service, customers are willing to pay a premium that is beneficial to both parties: the customer's savings far exceed the additional costs and the suppliers obtain a premium price for doing what they should have been doing in the first place.

The second major area is the integration of computer systems between customers and suppliers. In department stores, for example, the usage of stock items is automatically recorded. At suitable trigger points, orders are placed with the suppliers, goods are delivered, invoiced, and paid for all without the involvement of repetitive human activities.

These trends have transformed the traditional adversarial customer–supplier relationship into a long-term *partnership* with greater interdependence.

Desire to concentrate on own mainstream activities

In the past, companies tried to do most activities in-house. But they found that many tasks required professional skills that were not available inside the company, and a great deal of management time was diverted into these activities. More recently these peripheral activities have been subcontracted to specialist companies who handle these tasks on behalf of the customer, either on the customer's own premises or elsewhere. This again requires a complete customer orientation in the supplier's company. Catering services are a typical example of this trend.

THE ROLE OF THE FIRST-LINE MANAGER

As we have seen earlier, customer care is partially a matter of skills, processes and tools, and partially a question of attitudes. In both these areas, the first-line manager has a crucial role to play to ensure that senior management's intentions are suitably translated into actions where it really matters—where activities take place.

Your main tasks in orienting the company towards customer care are

◆ helping to identify the needs of your customers and understanding your company's desired position in the market.

◆ identifying strengths and deficiencies in your staff's customer skills.

◆ ensuring that deficiencies are remedied (by training, counseling, reorganization, reorientation) and that you build on strengths.

- establishing which processes and practices impede proper customer care and replacing them with customer-oriented systems.

- examining current measuring systems to ensure they monitor customer satisfaction.

- recognizing and rewarding good customer care performance.

- identifying issues in the process that impede good customer care and ensuring that these obstacles are removed.

- listening to customers, staff, colleagues, and senior management and communicating on customer issues.

- leading staff by example.

- motivating staff to achieve customer satisfaction goals.

This list could go on and on, but most of your tasks could probably be classified under one or the other of the above points. One of the difficulties companies have with implementing these tasks is that the authority vested in a first-line manager is often not sufficient to carry out all the above tasks efficiently.

Senior managers have plenty of problems of their own and are not looking for additional ones. They will be much more willing to support any action proposed by you if you can present to them not only the problem, but also a proposed resolution. Where other functions are involved, you should discuss the issues with them beforehand, and then present an agreed upon proposal to senior management.

We will see in Chapter 2 that company activities in various departments are closely interlinked; close cooperation among the various functions is essential to achieve a highly customer-orientated approach and present to the customer a seamless organization. The impetus must come from all the areas that can identify an improvement in customer support.

In this context we should mention that company staff in direct contact with the customer (salespeople, service engineers, telephonists, delivery staff, secretaries) are often very well aware of the lack of customer support provided by the company. Their suggestions, however, are frequently not sought, and even where they are, they are sometimes ignored. If you give the matter a little thought, you will realize that these intelligent individuals, who are in daily contact with customers, are likely to be a very useful source of information about customer needs and of suggestions about how these requirements can be met. It is your role to tap into this valuable source for improving customer care by involving staff in discussions on this subject (we will learn more about this in Chapter 4).

YOUR ORGANIZATION

The subjects discussed in this chapter form the framework for the issues we will examine more closely throughout the rest of the book. Perhaps now is a good time for you to look at your organization, and specifically your department, and ask yourself a number of pertinent questions.

◆ Have you clearly defined what customer care means in your business?

◆ Are you aware that doing your work as efficiently as possible is not only adding to your company's profit but also to customer satisfaction, which will keep your company in business?

◆ Do you genuinely believe in the "Customer is King" adage or are these only empty words?

◆ Are you concentrating only on your products or services, or do you analyze all your activities from the customer's point of view?

◆ When you look at the improvements introduced over the past two years, have they been generated primarily by internal needs or have they been customer oriented? Can you think of other improvements that will increase customer satisfaction?

◆ What are you doing to provide your staff with the relevant skills and aids needed for their job?

◆ Is the environment in your company conducive to a positive staff attitude towards the company?

◆ Do you think you can compete effectively in a rapidly changing market without making radical changes in the way you view customers?

◆ How has your own role changed over the past two years and how is it likely to change in the near future? How much effort is going into customer-oriented thinking?

◆ How well do you communicate? With customers? Within your department? With other functions? With senior managers?

Thinking about these issues now will help you apply what you will learn in the remaining chapters of the book.

Chapter 2

Who Are the Customers?

Yesterday we examined customer care and its impact on profits. We also established the reasons for its growing importance and why action to improve customer care is required *now*. We found that the first-line manager has a crucial role to play in involving top management and motivating her staff to develop and implement an effective customer support program.

In this chapter you will learn to:

◆ Identify your customers, which can be in three categories:

1. the *internal* customer.

2. the *external* customer (sometimes the *end use* customer).

3. the *end use* customer, or *consumer.*

◆ establish customer needs.

◆ recognize everyone's role in customer care.

◆ use customer support as a competitive tool.

WHO IS MY CUSTOMER?

Don't dismiss this simple question without giving it a little thought. The immediate response is likely to be the end user of your product. On the path from the design of a product, through its various stages of manufacturing, testing, packaging, distribution, storing, selling, invoicing, installing, servicing, collecting payment, and so on, there is a long chain of activities. Each activity is performed by an individual or a group of individuals, and the output of this activity is used by someone else in the chain. Each recipient of this output *is a customer* and must be viewed just like an outside customer or end user.

Internal customers

It may not be easy to change your attitude toward your colleagues by considering them to be your customers or your suppliers, whichever the case may be. But, if you want to support the end user adequately (and in Chapter 1 we established the essential need to do just that) then you cannot ignore the intermediate links in the chain.

Staff in direct contact with customers cannot provide good service to them unless they in turn are efficiently supported by their colleagues along the chain. You train your staff who are in direct contact with outside customers and end users in customer care skills. By using the same customer care skills on each and every internal customer, you will strengthen the whole chain, which will enable you to offer the end user more complete support. The chain is only as strong as its weakest link.

You may accept that idea conceptually but you may have some difficulty in converting it into action. One reason for this hesitation may well be that it has not been done previously. Well, don't hesitate! It is much easier to identify internal customers and to establish their needs than to do so for outside customers.

Who then is your internal customer? Just ask yourself the question "Who uses the output of my work?" and you have the answer. Everyone who uses the output of your work is your customer, be that person inside the company or an external user. Consequently, you probably have a number of customers with possibly different needs and priorities.

External customers

It is not only the end user who is your customer. But there are often a number of intermediary customers who have needs that have to be satisfied. These intermediaries can be agents, distributors, wholesalers, retailers, or other types of middlemen. Needs of all these customers must be satisfied.

End Use Customer

The customer, or consumer, is the end user of your product. It is this end use customer who pays for the product or the service, and who is therefore the most important of all your customers. His needs must be kept in the forefront of everyone's mind who is involved with providing the product or service.

Examples of Internal, External, and End Use Customers

Let's say you are in the aircraft component manufacturing business as a design engineer. Your immediate customer is the production engineer whom you must work with and satisfy that your design can be easily and inexpensively manufactured. The production engineer's customer is the shop foreman whose shop will manufacture your design. The production engineer must assure the shop foreman that his proposed manufacturing methods and the tools he will provide will allow the shop to produce a high quality, satisfactory product. The shop foreman's customer is the marketing manager who will sell and ship the product to her customer, the aircraft manufacturer. The aircraft manufacturer will then install your product on their aircraft, and sell the entire package to their customer, the airline. The airline will then, using this aircraft, provide a service to their customers, the passengers.

However, it is pretty clear that the design engineer must also consider the aircraft manufacturer, the airline, and the airline's customers' needs when designing his product. He must treat them all as customers. The aircraft manufacturer will desire a design that is low cost, light in weight, and easy to install on the aircraft. The airline will want a product that is designed to be easy to maintain and have a long life between failures. The entire aircraft, including your product, has been created for the convenience of the end user, the airline passenger, who, although she may not be aware of the existence of your product, enjoys the product's contribution to the safety, convenience, and affordable transportation that she is being offered.

In this scenario, the production engineer, the shop foreman, and the marketing manager are all *internal customers*. The aircraft manufacturer and the airline are both *external customers*. The airline passenger is the *end use customer*, or *consumer*.

IDENTIFYING CUSTOMER NEEDS

Now that you have clearly established who your customers really are, you must proceed to find out their genuine and perceived needs. Where internal customers are concerned you should first of all separate their *needs* from their *wishes* and, by agreement with them, set about satisfying their genuine needs and setting aside the "it would be nice to have" items. When it comes to external customers, whether they be the end users or intermediaries, it may be beneficial to satisfy both their real and perceived needs, as you may be able to gain a competitive advantage by catering to their perceived requirements as well, which may enable you to charge a premium price.

How do you identify these needs? The obvious answer is to ask your customers and discuss their needs with them, so that you clearly understand what they really want. For this purpose it will be advantageous if you know as much about your customers' business as possible.

It is much easier to have this type of dialogue with an internal customer and yet we often fail to communicate adequately and in sufficient detail with our colleagues. The company frequently spends a great deal of effort and money in establishing end use customer needs while ignoring the much simpler task of finding out exactly what one person (or department) requires from another. Yet unless the internal processes work satisfactorily, a favorable external result will be difficult to achieve.

This dialogue with your internal customers should result in a very clear specification of what the output of your work should be, its timing, frequency, amount of detail, and to what standard the work should comply (see Chapter 6). This specification should be reviewed at regular intervals, as changing conditions may affect internal customers' requirements. For instance, it often happens that a statistical report or sales results are needed very frequently in the early stages of a product launch, but a longer interval between reports may be quite adequate at a later stage. If requirements are not regularly reviewed, company resources may be wasted.

Establishing external and end use customers' needs is somewhat more complex as, in many cases, it will not be possible to ask each customer individually what his or her requirements are. A whole range of approaches is available:

◆ direct discussion with customers

◆ feedback from staff

◆ analysis of customer complaints and comments (see Chapter 5)

◆ market research

◆ surveys

◆ questionnaires (written, by telephone, personal interviews)

◆ user-group discussions

◆ customer audits

◆ attitude surveys

◆ VIP visits to the premises

These alternatives can be used singly or in conjunction with one another and in some cases (e.g., attitude surveys) the trends are more important than the absolute figures.

Some companies are concerned that their customers will not be willing to discuss their needs with them. In practice, customers are only too willing to let you have this information if they believe that you will utilize it. It is up to you to build a sufficiently good relationship with your customers for them to feel that you are sincere in your desire to satisfy their needs.

The quality of customer responses is likely to be varied. It is essential for these responses to be carefully analyzed and, wherever appropriate, specific customer issues should be addressed immediately and progress communicated to the customer.

The same need for prompt response exists where we you received feedback from your staff. Unless you keep the originator of the information fully informed on how the data has been used and what action you intend to take (or the reason for no action) the feedback will dry up. Because the feedback is so important, you must ensure a continuous flow of information by showing your appreciation to your staff.

The quest for updating your knowledge of customer needs, applications, and satisfaction is never ending and continually changing. These changing requirements are influenced by the changing needs of your customers' markets and by the enhanced offerings provided by your competitors and yourselves. Yesterday's outstanding performance becomes today's standard and will be unacceptable tomorrow. If you want to succeed in your aim to delight customers, you will have to try to stay at least one step ahead of the competition.

EVERYONE HAS A ROLE IN CUSTOMER CARE
Hopefully everyone in the company produces an output that is useful to someone else, either inside or outside the company. If not, then maybe the job in question is superfluous. It is therefore necessary to recognize that each person's work contributes to the whole package of activities that makes the customer want to continue doing business with you.

USING CUSTOMER SUPPORT AS A COMPETITIVE TOOL
It is not enough to provide excellent customer support—you also have to make it known to customers that you are doing so. Why is that necessary? Surely customers will know when they get superior service. It is a fact, however, that customer support is more apparent to customers by its absence than by its presence. Customers tend to take good customer support for granted, although experience should have taught them that this is not always the case.

Companies who provide good support have in the past few years learned to be forthcoming in letting existing customers, as well as potential new ones, know that the company takes customer support seriously. The way this has been done includes programs such as:

◆ customer charters.

◆ extended warranties.

◆ clearly stated performance standards.

◆ acceptance of penalties for noncompliance.

◆ return of money if the customer is not satisfied.

◆ publicity given to support provided.

◆ additional free services (e.g., loaner cars during maintenance of customer's vehicle).

◆ customer helplines—carelines (see Chapter 6), 800-number freebies.

It is becoming increasingly popular for key customers to be invited to act as a third-party reference in publicity material to highlight the benefit the customer has obtained by the support of the supplier. The partnership approach between customer and supplier is stressed. This is not only an excellent third-party reference for the supplier but, in addition, a good sales aid in the key customer's company, as the benefit of the support is brought home to a wide range of people in the customer's organization, who may never have been involved with the support.

The difficulty quite often is with your own staff who take the excellent support you provide for granted, but do not adequately stress its benefit to the external customer. It almost appears as if they are afraid of being boastful. Salesmen in one company, for instance, found it difficult to get an external customer to agree to let his staff be trained free of charge in the supplier's local premises; they were concerned that the customer might object to releasing his staff for a day's training. Other salesmen in the same company used this training as a positive selling point, stressing that the moment the customer's new equipment was installed on his premises, his staff would be ready to use it, and that the staff would make their mistakes on the supplier's equipment and not on the customer's newly installed one.

The bottom line is that customer support not only needs to be provided but it also needs to be sold and marketed to achieve maximum return for your company.

SUMMARY

In this chapter you have

◆ identified your internal, external, and end use customers.

◆ learned to establish customer needs.

◆ recognized the benefit of feedback from your staff.

◆ come to realize that everyone in the company should be involved in customer care.

◆ examined ways of selling and marketing the benefits of superior customer support to existing and potential customers.

Chapter 3

Elements That Influence Customer Care

In Chapter 2 you learned to identify your customers along the whole chain of activities that help you to support the end users. We examined ways of identifying customer needs and how to use customer support as a positive selling and marketing tool.

In this chapter we will go a step further and study

◆ the elements influencing customer care.

◆ customer care skills and attitudes.

◆ procedures and systems to assist you in customer care activities.

ELEMENTS INFLUENCING CUSTOMER CARE

As we saw in Chapter 1, the products provided by companies competing in any market are essentially similar and becoming more so every day. Customers' purchasing decisions are, therefore, influenced by elements other than the basic product. This is often referred to as the "nonproduct value added" and comprises all the factors that go into demonstrating genuine care for the customer. It is a meaningful description of customer care, because it adds value to the customer beyond that of your product.

Let us first enumerate these elements and then examine each one in greater detail.

◆ major purchases (external and end use customers)

◆ the way the initial contact is handled

◆ the follow-up process

◆ clear specification of product, features, price, payment terms, warranties, availability, and after-sales support

◆ simple ordering procedure

◆ prompt order acknowledgment restating specification and terms

◆ adherence to stated conditions

◆ advance notice of any necessary deviation from conditions

◆ assistance when product is delivered

◆ clear invoicing—no hidden charges

◆ easy access to supplier for assistance

◆ opportunity to extend warranty, making service contract or other after-sales service activity

◆ occasional after-sales contact

◆ all staff to be polite and helpful

These are just some of the most important elements applicable to all businesses. Can you think of additional ones applicable in your environment?

Initial contact

A great deal of tact is required by your staff to ensure that the customers realize they are being helped without getting the feeling of being pressurized by the salesperson. The initial contact by customers could have been made personally (e.g., in a shop, or by inviting an insurance salesperson to visit the customer), in writing by fax or letter, or by telephone. In all instances, your company should have clearly laid down standards on how this very important first contact should be handled (see Chapter 6). The first impression given to the customers at the time of the initial contact is likely to remain with them for a very long time and any bad impression will be difficult to eradicate.

Sometimes the first impression is created even before the customer starts talking to a member of your staff. Aspects that may influence this impression include cleanliness of premises, environment of the reception area, and customer parking facilities.

Not only do operational staff need to be trained in customer handling skills but top management and first-line management must also think "customer."

The follow-up process

Once the initial contact with customers has been made, you must ensure that any queries that may subsequently arise can be adequately dealt with by staying in touch with the customer. The same comment concerning the need for tact mentioned above applies. Customers must not get the feeling that you are pressurizing them as this would result in the customer's genuine queries and concerns not surfacing but being hidden by delaying tactics. The time after the initial contact is crucial, as customers are undecided and, in many cases, confused about their own requirements and whether the supplier's product can satisfy even the known needs.

This is the time to convert the customer's fears of making the wrong decision into conviction that your product and its support is what is needed. Helpful advice can effect a positive decision. Knowledge of the customer's products, industry, and processes can be of immense help in enabling you to give customers confidence in the advice you are giving. This is why an increasing number of suppliers have industry-specific teams of experts to advise customers and potential customers. An honest approach is essential.

Clear specifications

Nothing is likely to annoy customers more than specifications of products and features that are vague or unclear, either deliberately or through carelessness. The same applies to pricing and payment terms, where some suppliers try to hide the fact that "extras" are not standard equipment and have to be paid for separately. Even if customers do not complain, it leaves a bad taste in their mouths and they may not return to you for future purchases.

Warranties have also become a significant marketing tool in certain industries, and clear identification of what is and what is not included in the warranty is essential. The sale of extended warranties and other support activities, which become effective after expiration of the initial warranty, are becoming an increasingly profitable area of a manufacturer's or supplier's product palette, and here again, an absolutely clear statement of what is covered is essential.

A realistic date for availability and delivery must be given to customers. Overoptimistic statements of delivery time will have a detrimental effect on the supplier's image in customers' eyes and may lead to major upsets. This is particularly important on products or services that tie into other activities or needs of customers.

Simple ordering procedure

This seems like an obvious point, but examine the difficulties some companies seem to put deliberately in the way of customers wishing to place an order. In some instances, customers cannot use their own ordering procedures, but are asked to conform to those of their suppliers. They may have to complete complicated forms seeking unimportant information, which may have been useful in the past but is of no conceivable use now.

Prompt order acknowledgment

The least you, as suppliers, can do to show gratitude to customers for having chosen you as suppliers, is to acknowledge the order promptly and to state clearly on it your understanding of what the customer ordered. This acknowledgment should leave no need for the customer to query it or for any vagueness that could lead to subsequent disputes.

Adherence to conditions

It almost goes without saying that it is essential to adhere to the terms and conditions agreed with the customer on the order and its acknowledgment. Customers have a genuine cause for complaint if you, the suppliers, do not respect the conditions and specifications of the order. Incidentally, it has been found by research that, where conditions are strictly adhered to, the customers tend to pay more promptly and will be more likely to keep to the payment terms.

Advance notice of necessary deviation from conditions

On some rare occasions it may be impossible for you, as suppliers, to meet all the conditions. One typical deviation is a delivery promise that, for some reason or other, cannot be met. The essential part of customer care is not to wait till you have missed the promised delivery date (perhaps in the hope that the customer will not notice?) but to contact the customer immediately when you find out that you cannot meet the promised date. This will enable a solution to be agreed on between the customer and yourself to minimize any problem that your missing the delivery date is likely to cause the customer.

Contacting customers before the event will also take the steam out of the situation as the customers will realize that you care about any problems you may cause.

Assistance when a product is delivered

Some companies believe their task is completed when the product is delivered to the customer. This may be true in many industries, but in a number of others the customer needs advice or other help to become familiar with the product he has just bought. This assistance may take the form of training a customer's staff on how to operate the product, or it may require physical or verbal help in assembling the product to get it operational.

Operating manuals and installation instructions are often very difficult to follow, and in some cases, manufacturers have clearly not field-tested their manuals or instructions on consumers. Customer care includes the supplier ensuring that the introduction of the product to a customer's premises proceeds as smoothly as possible.

Clear invoicing

Here again a clear statement of what the customer is asked to pay for is essential. Great improvements have been made over the past few years, but there are still invoices that give only codes that are comprehensible to the supplier but meaningless to customers. There are supermarket printouts that do not itemize purchases or, worst of all, invoices that try to confuse the customer in the hope that she will not query extras, which she may have had a right to assume would be part of the basic price. Often queries directed to the invoicing department are answered by staff who have not been trained in how to deal with customers and who consider a call by a customer an interruption of their "real" work. Staff in these departments must clearly understand that it is the customer who pays all their salaries, and management must ensure that staff are properly trained.

Easy access to the supplier

Customers must be able to contact the supplier not only when they have an inquiry prior to purchasing a product, but also after the sale. This is an area where immense progress has been made by a number of progressive companies through encouraging customers to contact them by providing help centers, hotlines, and other tools that enable customers to voice their opinions, get assistance, and feel that the company is genuinely interested in assisting them. We will discuss these tools in greater detail in Chapter 6.

Opportunity to contract additional services

Customers are increasingly calculating the life-cycle costs of a product. They probably received meaningful data about the acquisition cost, running costs, and other expenses involved in the early stages of a product, but they may find it beneficial to be able to obtain from the supplier information about extended warranties or service contracts (that can be considered as an insurance cover against expensive repair costs). They may also require information about other after-sales maintenance alternatives (e.g., time and material, exchange of modules) or about advance training of their staff in operating the equipment to its full potential, or in performing simple maintenance tasks themselves.

Occasional after-sales contact

After customers have taken delivery of a product, suppliers often forget about the original customer in their drive to find additional customers. The customer feels abandoned by the supplier. An occasional contact by the supplier will strengthen ties between customers and suppliers, and when it comes to upgrading the customer's product or to additional purchases, this pampering of the customer will show a worthwhile payoff. This customer care activity will also favorably affect the attitude of the customer toward the supplier, which will be useful when using the customer as a reference.

Dealing with customers

Although it should be obvious that all staff in contact with customers must at all times be polite and helpful, this is not always the case. Management must ensure that this prerequisite to good customer relations is clearly understood by everyone in the company. As we will see in Chapter 5, the attitude of staff will be strongly influenced by their attitude towards their employer. Staff attitude, in turn, will be reflected in the way they communicate with customers.

CONSUMER PURCHASES

Friendly response to order

Customers always respond to a friendly face, a friendly approach, whether the customer is buying a hamburger or an alarm clock, and will probably return to such a supplier for their other needs.

Helpful explanations

A helpful explanation, whether it be about the choices on a dinner menu or what software to buy to meet your needs, boosts customer loyalty and repeat sales.

Assistance when product is delivered

Most customers appreciate assistance when the product is delivered, such as store staff installing or setting up an appliance.

Replacement of defective product

A friendly, helpful, immediate offer to replace an apparently defective product without question will develop strong store or product loyalty and repeat sales.

CUSTOMER CARE SKILLS AND ATTITUDES

To ensure a continuous high level of customer care, a persistent management and staff effort over time is required. It cannot be dictated from above (although it must be driven by management) nor can it be introduced on short notice as a temporary measure. This is why organizations and brands try to differentiate themselves from their competitors by the quality of their customer care—it takes a long time and a great deal of effort to emulate the best practices of competitors. Customer care has to become an integral part of the organization's thinking. Where specific problems are identified, companies often try crash programs to alleviate the situation, but these measures are usually only temporarily effective.

The approach should be a disciplined, well-thought-out, step-by-step progression:

◆ develop and publish a statement of the organization's mission

◆ incorporate customer care as an integral part of the strategy

◆ prepare detailed plans of how to satisfy and exceed customers' identified needs

◆ employ staff with positive attitudes and further improve their customer handling skills

Mission statement

The nature of mission statements (or statements of company philosophy) means that they must come from top management. The important issue here is that management must recognize that customer care is an essential part of reaching a company's profit targets and thus of the very existence of an organization.

A study by two researchers, Frederick Harmon and Gary Jacobs, into the profitability of companies in their industrial groupings in the Fortune 500 list of companies showed that companies who had customer satisfaction as a priority issue in their mission statement were more profitable over a period of five years than companies who placed profitability at the top of their list. Many major organizations have used this study to review the visibility of customer satisfaction in their mission statement.

The crux, however, is not what management says, but how it acts to prove that the mission statement is not a mere platitude.

Incorporating customer care into the strategy

As we have just said, it is the *actions* of management that influence the attitudes of people inside and outside the company. It is therefore necessary to integrate customer care thinking in all company strategies. Top management must be involved in this activity to ensure that company resources are appropriately directed to support these strategies.

Incorporating customer-oriented considerations in all strategies does not mean that all decisions made by management will be popular with customers. For instance, it may from time to time be necessary to increase prices, which is bound to be unpopular with customers. What is important in these circumstances is for the customer to realize that he is still getting good value for money. Often your own staff are more resistant to a price increase than customers. The way you communicate the need for this increase to customers and to your staff affects its acceptability.

Developing detailed plans

To enable you to achieve the goals set out in the mission and in the strategy, you need to develop detailed plans on how to satisfy and exceed customers' identified needs. Here the full involvement of staff from all areas of the company will be helpful. It is these employees, who are closer to the day-to-day tasks they perform, who will be able to contribute ideas for improvements in their field of expertise, which may help to affect customers' satisfaction with what you are providing to them.

These plans need to be developed across all functions so that improvements in one area do not unfavorably affect others, unless this is a calculated decision that will benefit the customer or your company. For instance, some companies have decided to reduce the number of their warehouses, which increases their transportation cost substantially. However, the resulting benefit was an improved level of logistic support to customers and lower total costs to the supplier. As you can see, first-line management has a responsibility to involve top management in their strategy to accomplish major actions such as these and bring about an overall benefit to the customer. We will discuss developing customer care programs and plans in Chapter 7.

Employing staff with positive attitudes and imparting customer handling skills

Greater emphasis is being placed in the recruiting process to ensure newly engaged staff have the right attitude towards the company and towards customers. In most instances, you also have existing staff, some of whom may have the right attitudes, whereas others may require guidance. Attitudes cannot be taught by management but management can positively (or otherwise) influence existing attitudes.

What can and must be taught are customer handling skills. Like most other activities, there are accepted ways of doing this, although these may differ in some detail from culture to culture, or even from industry to industry. In the past, companies have taught customer handling skills only to salespeople, who by the nature of their job are probably most familiar with how to deal with customers. More recently, customer handling skills are being taught to other staff in companies, including especially service technicians, receptionists, telephone operators, and accounting staff, as well as other administrative staff who may be involved in some contact with customers.

Procedures and systems

To complete the circle, company procedures and systems must also be made more customer and operator friendly. Staff will not be able to satisfy customer needs if the tools at their disposal do not allow them to do this efficiently (more about this in Chapter 6). This means that internal procedures have to be viewed from the customer's point of view, and systems supporting these procedures must make them a real aid to assist your staff in helping customers and potential customers in their dealings with your company.

The personal touch in dealing with customers should be encouraged wherever possible, and certain information in the database should enable your staff to make customers feel like individuals, even though they may be dealing with a large organization where they are used to being treated as a number. An insurance executive stated at a seminar that research carried out by her company had shown that customers who had dealings with the insurance company found that the *way* their issues were processed was almost as important as the outcome itself. Don't let outdated procedures spoil your customer-oriented image.

SUMMARY

This chapter identified a number of elements that influence the way customers regard your company and examined each one of these factors more closely.

You have to *work* at changing attitudes and at imparting and reinforcing customer handling skills in a wide range of your staff.

Top management has to initiate and support customer-oriented activities, and four steps must be taken before you can effectively implement a customer care program.

Finally, internal procedures and systems need to be reviewed from time to time to make them more customer and operator friendly.

Chapter 4

Enhancing Customer Relations

We spent the last chapter learning about the elements that influence customer care. These elements can only be implemented by staff exhibiting the right attitudes, having been taught the requisite skills to deal effectively with customers, and being supported by customer-friendly processes and systems.

In this chapter we will study ways of

◆ enhancing customer relations.

◆ improving communications:
  – written
  – telecommunication
  – personal

◆ developing a seamless organization—the team approach.

ENHANCING CUSTOMER RELATIONS

Your company goal should be to create relationships with customers that will not only satisfy their immediate needs, but that will leave customers with a feeling of goodwill towards the supplier. This feeling will make them want to continue doing business with the supplier and sing praises of the supplier to the world in general.

This type of long-term relationship must be built on mutual trust and respect, which are created by adhering to the concepts learned yesterday.

Customers want to have relationships that will continue for a considerable time, where the supplier knows the customer's needs and the customer can rely on the supplier's assistance if and when required.

Let us assume the customer is a car manufacturer who purchases electric motors from a vendor. The electrical systems of a car on the drawing board today must be developed in parallel with the rest of the car. Who is likely to know more about electric motors, the car manufacturer or the manufacturer of the electric motors? It is therefore highly desirable to have the specialists from the manufacturer of electric motors working together with the designers of the car to come up with an optimal solution. This will, however, mean divulging sensitive information to each other and there must be complete confidence on both sides that the other will not use this information for improper purposes.

This frankness in a partnership relationship is not confined to technical information, it also often covers other areas of business, including finance. It has been known for financially strong customers to advance grants or loans to vendors for, perhaps, capital investment in new machinery of a computing system, which uses the same architecture as that of the customer, to simplify administrative procedures on both sides.

To ensure all staff really enhance the relationship with customers, suppliers go to substantial lengths to check that the procedures and standards laid down are fully complied with. To demonstrate that their procedures are able to provide customers with the agreed standards, many companies seek ISO 9000 accreditation.

Company executives are sometimes surprised when they call their offices and telephones are inappropriately answered, some calls are carelessly transferred to wrong departments, or the impatience of the receptionist or other recipient of the phone call is apparent from the person's voice. Some companies have made it a firm requirement for *all* executives, including the chief executive officer, to spend part of their time out in the field talking to customers and staff at the sharp end of the business. As one executive remarked, "We cannot make meaningful strategic decisions about our business if we do not know what it is like to face customers." In some companies senior executives from various disciplines are allocated a number of key customers with whom they keep in regular contact.

The mystery-shopper approach is used by a number of organizations to check compliance to customer care procedures. This can be done either by the company's own staff or by employing an outside company to check a range of preselected factors regularly in the customer relations field.

As we have seen, enhancing customer relations consists of a number of tangible elements and intangible elements that make customers feel comfortable in dealing with your company.

COMMUNICATION

Let us first define communication. Perhaps it is easiest to first state what communication is not. The passing of information in a single direction (e.g., an instruction down the line, or a report up the line) is highly important, but it is not communication. Communication is multidirectional or, at least, two directional.

The danger of simply passing information from one person, one department, or one organization to another is that the information may be misunderstood or misinterpreted, or be taken out of the context intended by the initiator.

Communication helps to eliminate, or at least minimize, any possible misunderstanding through the recipient's comments and the feedback received by the initiator. What is more, it is likely to lead to much more involvement in the common task by all persons concerned, which in turn will lead to better decisions, greater commitment, and thus more rapid and thorough implementation. In addition it is also motivational (see Chapter 5).

Let us examine ways we tend to communicate.

◆ by exchange of letters, faxes, or e-mail

◆ by telecommunications

◆ by personal contact

Exchange of letters, faxes, or e-mail

By the nature of this method of communication, the interchange of ideas and feelings is somewhat stilted and limited by the absence of an immediate response and of nonverbal indicators (e.g., smiles, hand movements, shrugs, and other expressions conveying the other person's feelings). Nevertheless, this written method gives the initiator the opportunity to review the message carefully before sending it, and there is a permanent record of it. Often letters and faxes are used to confirm an understanding reached by other methods of communication to combine the advantages of more than one way of communicating.

Telecommunication

This is a much more spontaneous way of communicating, as the interchange is instantaneous and the tone of voice helps to convey some of the feelings that may not be expressed in words. Because of this spontaneity, it is used increasingly in business, and the improvement in wired as well as in cellular systems is making the telephone an essential part of communicating with people inside and outside the company (see also Chapter 6).

The disadvantage of the telephone for communication purposes is the absence of visual contact and the possibility that the recipient of your call will be caught unawares or be distracted by other activities in the office (or by traffic on the road if you reach the recipient while he or she is traveling). Also, there is no written record of the exchange of information, although in some organizations all telephone calls are randomly recorded (with appropriate notification given to the caller).

By personal contact

This is the oldest and most effective way of communicating with your staff and with customers and vendors. It is spontaneous, there is visual as well as audio contact, and there is a clear feedback of understanding or the lack of it.

Although there is generally no permanent record of the discussion (except where minutes are taken or a record is specifically requested by one or other of the parties), the outcome can be easily confirmed in a subsequent letter or fax. The main drawback of personal contact is the time and travel expense required for this method of communication.

Videoconferencing combines the advantages of personal contact with reducing the time and cost involved in traveling, but it is still a somewhat artificial way of making personal contact.

In many cases real communication takes place in a nonformal relaxed setting after office hours, such as at a lunch or dinner when people get to know each other better and are more willing to talk one on one.

Each of these methods of communication requires specific skills that you must teach your staff. Some of these skills (e.g., clarity and conciseness of expression) are common to all, others are specific to each method. It would involve too much detail to cover these skills in this book. Suffice it to say that material on all these skills is widely available. Here we are concerned with recognizing the need to impart these communication skills to staff.

One aspect that should be stressed is the real need to *listen* to the other party, be it a customer, a member of your staff, or anybody else. This means not only *hearing* (or reading) what the other party says, but trying to understand the intent of the communication and to take the idea on board. Too often the words are heard but the idea is dismissed without full consideration. What we hear is also colored by our experience and preconceived ideas so that we make no serious effort to consider the real intent of the message. I used to consider myself a good listener until I took a listening course. In the first hour of that course, it was proved to all participants that their perceptions colored what they thought they had heard.

Ten suggestions to improve listening

1. Listen for ideas, not just for words or reactions to persons.

2. Take notes.

3. Ask questions.

4. Switch off your problems.

5. Limit your talking.

6. Don't interrupt.

7. Think like the customer.

8. Don't jump to conclusions.

9. Listen to overtones.

10. Concentrate.

It is estimated that 75 percent of a manager's time is spent communicating. This time is divided, as per recent studies, approximately as follows:

Listening	*45–60 percent*
Reading	*4–19 percent*
Talking	*21–51 percent*

This demonstrates the benefit of making some effort to improve your listening skills.

In this context, remember that communication conveyed by more than one sense is more likely to be remembered; it is therefore beneficial to combine the same message through a number of senses (e.g., through verbal communication and visual confirmation).

With the increasing use of the telephone mentioned earlier, many organizations are concentrating their training in this area. Precise guidelines are prepared on how the initial call should be answered, how it is to be transferred if this should become necessary, and the degree of formality that they wish to be used by their staff on the telephone.

For some unexplained reason, time wasted in waiting for the telephone to be answered or transferred is more aggravating than other types of delays. Therefore, this needs to be avoided by careful monitoring and planning. We will explore this subject further in Chapter 6.

THE TEAM APPROACH

In today's complex business world it is often necessary to utilize experts in a number of different technical, financial, marketing, sales, administrative, or other professional fields to enable us to serve the customer adequately. The customers, however, want to obtain an integrated recommendation from us covering all areas of expertise. Companies have realized this customer requirement for some time and have used specialists in various fields to assist the customer.

The difficulty that these companies experienced was the uncoordinated approach of all these experts, as each one advised the customer on the best approach relevant to his functional expertise, leaving the customer more confused than ever. Part of the problem was the functional organizational structure in most companies, and the allegiance members of particular functions had to their departments.

To overcome this difficulty, companies' top managements are increasingly structuring their organizations to reflect the customers' needs rather than their own internal requirements. This has meant creating teams of people from various specialized areas to work together on a customer project and present the customer with genuine solutions to problems. These teams are formed and disbanded as the needs dictated by customers' requirements arise. These more flexible structures give customers a seamless image of a unified approach from the supplier.

Managing these teams from different professional disciplines requires a completely different management style. The professional guidance of team members is provided by someone outside the team whereas the (temporary) team manager may not have the professional functional skills of the individual team member. The team manager will, however, be very knowledgeable about the customers' industry and the specific needs of individual customers.

The skill of the manager is increasingly involved with encouraging (or motivating) team members to work together for the benefit of the end result, which is to satisfy the customer and thus create additional profit for the company. The length of time team members will work together will differ depending on the type and extent of the project. The team may well consist of a number of permanent members and others that are co-opted for specific tasks for limited periods of time. Clearly, the difficult task of the team managers is to keep all resources and efforts devoted towards reaching the end goal.

In the next chapter we will discuss some ways managers can motivate their staff or team members.

As in a football team, the strength of the team is dependent not only on the skills of the individual players but also on how well they work together. In the same way a project team must be fully integrated into the effort of supporting the customers' projects and must not press ahead with narrow, internal functional preferences to the detriment of the end result.

SUMMARY

This chapter concentrated on enhancing customer relations and the essential role played in this area by communication with customers, vendors, and your staff.

We examined these methods of communication in some detail and identified advantages and disadvantages in each one of them. Whenever really important information needs to be exchanged, a combination of methods is beneficial. Strained customer relations are often caused by an omission of concerted management action.

We detailed the reasons why teamwork has become essential in today's environment and we examined the current moves towards a more flexible, seamless organization. The task of managers in this flexible team structure has changed and necessitates a greater orientation towards customers.

Finally, top management must be involved in your customer care strategies in order to obtain the resources and company mind-set needed to accomplish your goals.

Chapter 5

Complaints

Chapter 4 examined ways of enhancing customer relations. We found that communication was an essential skill to use to keep customers happy and to form long-term partnerships with them. Yet customer dissatisfaction and complaints are sometimes inevitable.

This chapter examines

◆ complaints:
  – complaints handling
  – complaints management
  – the role of management

◆ motivation.

◆ brainstorming.

COMPLAINTS

In the past, management often tried to avoid complaints being made by customers and when they were being made, they were dealt with at a management level as far away as possible from senior management.

During the last decade or two, more and more companies have come to realize that complaints are a valuable way of establishing customer needs and hearing their opinions and comments about their products and services. Companies now tend to spend a great deal of money and effort to encourage customers to complain and comment.

Why has there been such a drastic change of approach to complaints? As we have seen earlier, it costs on average five times as much to acquire a new customer than it does to retain an existing one. Furthermore, existing customers tend to spend more with you than new customers, and they are likely to remain more loyal to your company or to your brand.

Other studies have shown that only a relatively small percentage of dissatisfied customers will actually make a complaint that would give you the opportunity to put matters right and turn them into satisfied customers. The great majority of customers will simply vote with their feet and not come back to you; they will, however, tell their friends and colleagues about their real or imagined grievance without giving you a chance to comment.

Encouraging customers to complain

Having come to the conclusion that you *want to encourage* customers to complain you have to find ways of doing so. Some companies go to extreme lengths and substantial costs to make it easy for customers to complain or make their views known. Here a few examples:

- stamped and addressed cards supplied with products or easily available at point of sale

- free phone help lines manned for long periods of the day

- customer service desks at point of sale

- approach after the sale by the supplier or manufacturer to the customer to check satisfaction

- offer of exchange or money back if not satisfied

Having initiated actions to encourage customers to complain, you must have a quick and easy follow-up procedure for dealing with these complaints. The actions you must take fall into two distinct areas: the handling of complaints and the management of complaints.

Handling complaints

This is the immediate action required to pacify the customer and to resolve, or at least mitigate, the issue. Customers are often almost as concerned about *how* their complaint is dealt with as they are with the final outcome itself. There are six basic rules to handling complaints:

- Listen.

- Probe.

- Agree on a solution.

- Adhere to the agreed-on solution.

- Follow up.

- Implement an escalation procedure if necessary.

LISTEN

Nothing is likely to make customers more angry than if the person they complain to does not pay full attention to what is being said or, worse still, interrupts on the assumption that the issue has already been understood. The message is *listen*, do not interrupt, take notes, and show sympathetic interest. Always remain calm and polite.

PROBE

The facts have to be established in some detail and it will usually be necessary to ask questions to avoid misunderstandings and to get the complete picture. In some instances, this questioning may resolve the issue by highlighting some action the customer may have omitted to take or clarifying an explanation that has been misinterpreted. The probing should proceed in a systematic way to enable the next step to be undertaken.

AGREE ON A SOLUTION

Having elicited all relevant facts, you are now in a position to propose a solution that is agreeable to the customer. You may not be able to resolve the issue completely on the spot, but you can probably find an interim solution that is acceptable to the customer until the matter is finally resolved. This agreed-on solution should be very specific, and it must not leave the customer in any doubt as to what to expect.

ADHERE TO THE AGREED-ON SOLUTION

You certainly do not want to irritate customers further by letting them down a second time. It is essential to ensure that every detail of the promised solution is fulfilled. It is not good enough simply to request another department to perform some action—you have taken on the responsibility on behalf of the company to take certain actions, and you must ensure that they happen. You have to get the firm commitment of any other person or department involved that the remedial action will be taken, and you must check that this is performed to the agreed standards and schedule.

FOLLOW UP

Once you have ensured that the agreed-on solution has been fully implemented, it is recommended practice for you to contact the customer again to get a positive agreement that you now have a satisfied customer again. A clear procedure must be laid down in your company to make sure that this additional step is taken to demonstrate your involvement with the customer's problem. Customers who have had a complaint and who have been fairly and quickly dealt with will become loyal clients in the future, and they will be happy to recommend your company to other potential customers.

ESCALATION PROCEDURE

It is not always possible to come to an agreed-on solution with a customer. Most customers are reasonable people to deal with, but there are always exceptions. For this reason, and because some issues may have to be resolved at a higher management level, escalation procedures should exist and should be implemented in all appropriate circumstances. However, you should empower your staff who are dealing with complaints, to enable them to come to a resolution with the customer on the spot. In a survey by British Airways, it was found that travelers who had a complaint wanted it resolved by the person they were talking to without having the matter referred to higher authority. The high priority given to this customer requirement in the survey was a surprise to the company, and a change was initiated as part of their customer care program.

Managing complaints

Once the immediate fire has been put out you must take further advantage of the complaint by examining the underlying cause of it to ensure it does not occur again. In the past, companies resisted this type of investigation as they felt that a witch hunt after the event was not going to bring them much benefit. With the recent drive for excellence, they have found it essential to establish the root cause of the complaint and to take appropriate action (even if that action is a considered decision not to take any action).

This is not as simple as it sounds in view of the fact that a number of different departments may be involved and their short-term priorities may be different from those of the person trying to resolve a complaint. That is the reason why top management and first-line management must develop, publish, and thoroughly implement procedures to ensure that issues are followed through to their logical conclusion.

The approach often taken is based on the team approach we examined in Chapter 4. Representatives of various departments involved form a team to study the basic cause of individual complaints and agree on solutions and their timing. This has led to substantial improvements in the operation of companies, which has more than paid for the costs involved in handling and managing complaints. It has also had the additional, nonquantified benefit of enhancing customer satisfaction, which brings with it consequent marketing advantages to the company.

The role of management

In well-run organizations, customer complaints are being taken very seriously. It is usual to have a senior executive take charge of coordinating all activities involved in handling and managing complaints (not necessarily on a full-time basis) and for her to have to report to the board of directors on various aspects pertinent to complaints on a regular basis.

MOTIVATION

This is a subject that behavioral scientists study all their lives and we will not attempt here to turn ourselves into specialists on motivation. However, we need to know how to apply motivational theories to the practical task of motivating customer care staff. Assume for now that in your company the "hygiene factors" (those factors that cause dissatisfaction among employees if the factors are inadequate or nonexistent but that will not positively motivate them if the factors are further improved) are satisfactory. You can only start motivating your staff once this stage has been reached.

Behavioral scientists agree that all of us are motivated by certain factors, but each one of us may have a different mix of priorities and motivators. Below is a list of some of the most important motivating factors.

◆ involvement

◆ achievement

◆ recognition

◆ feeling of belonging

Let us examine each of these in more detail to see how you can motivate your customer care staff.

Involvement

Everyone wants their ideas to be thought worthwhile and to be considered seriously. Managers often underestimate the wealth of knowledge and genuine interest of their employees. It is up to you, the manager, to harness this knowledge and to get your staff to put forward their ideas. You have to encourage your staff to do so actively. From past experience, employees know that managers tend to trivialize suggestions by their staff or, worse still, to ridicule the person who made the suggestion. This leads to a reticence from staff to put ideas forward publicly; instead, staff tend to grumble among themselves, adversely affecting morale.

To overcome this natural reticence and to release the potential inherent in your staff, you have to encourage them to get involved in generating ideas, to be willing to express their opinions freely and without fear of negative reactions from their managers or colleagues. Various formal and informal methods are used to encourage this involvement, but the most important one is the attitude of the individual manager and the whole management team—especially top management.

Once this attitude exists, the following methods are used singly or jointly by various companies to get their staff to contribute their ideas:

◆ small work-group meetings

◆ formal suggestion schemes

◆ quality circles

◆ brainstorming sessions

- ◆ managers' open-door policy

- ◆ cross-functional assignments

- ◆ managers talking and listening to their staff

- ◆ open communication flow

Achievement

We spend a great part of our waking life at work and we all want to take pride in what we do. To enable us to be proud of our work, we not only need the recognition of our managers and colleagues, but we also need to get a feeling of satisfaction at having achieved something worthwhile.

To enable you to recognize that you have achieved something, your goal must be clearly established. This goal should not only be a long-term target with, perhaps, a one-year time horizon, but should consist of short-term, intermediate goals or milestones against which you can measure yourself along the way.

One of the most widely used ways for employees to be able to get a feeling of achievement is a regular performance review by their manager. During this review the employee and the manager agree on performance targets and standards for the next period, and achievements since the last review are discussed. Targets should be challenging, but they must be achievable.

With the current drive for "flatter" organizational structures, there is a need for more genuine delegation by the manager, which is likely to have beneficial effects on the motivation of the employee. Delegation is a skill in its own right that you, as manager, must acquire. Delegation does not mean telling the employee step by step how the job should be done; that is instruction. Nor is it to throw a task at the employee and then ignore him until the task is completed; that is not delegation, that is abrogation. Genuine delegation means entrusting work to another person and assigning them responsibility and authority to do that work.

Recognition

Having achieved your goal, it is always pleasant to have one's achievements appreciated by others. Here again you, the manager, have a role to play. The most basic requirement is for recognition to be genuine (only real progress should be praised). The second desirable step is for recognition to be as public as possible. Keep to the dictum, "Praise in public and criticize in private." (So many of us tend to do exactly the opposite.) This can be done in a number of ways:

◆ at a group meeting

◆ publicizing a letter of appreciation on the notice board

◆ an article in the newsletter or company magazine

◆ arranging for a senior manager to congratulate the employee in front of the latter's colleagues

◆ naming a program or invention after the inventor

◆ inviting the employees with their spouses to a celebration

◆ monetary or in-kind awards

Feeling of belonging

This is a difficult one! This type of feeling cannot be generated on short notice. It is based on an attitude of trust by all levels of management—trust in their staff, which is usually reciprocated by the employee's loyalty to the company. It takes time to engender this type of an attitude but it can be destroyed quite quickly. Most people like to be team players; they want to belong to a group of which they can feel proud. It is your management task to build this team spirit to ensure everyone in the company is pulling in the same direction. Some of the methods used to generate a feeling of belonging include

◆ free communication and involvement.

◆ shedding the "them and us" distinction between management and staff.

◆ public recognition of achievement.

◆ company social and sports activities.

It is essential for each of your staff members to understand that managers' achievements are measurable as the sum of the achievements of all their staff, and thus everyone contributes with his or her performance to the end objective. Once this is understood, the constructive criticism by the manager will be more readily accepted as a move towards improvements desired by everyone concerned.

BRAINSTORMING

We mentioned brainstorming as one of the techniques that can be employed to encourage involvement of your employees in the company's activities. Let us examine some basic rules of brainstorming.

◆ Select people who can and are willing to contribute.

◆ Allow adequate time.

◆ Choose an appropriate subject and put it on a flip chart.

◆ Carefully explain that:
　– everyone is completely free to suggest ideas on the subject;
　– all ideas, however wild they may seem, should be contributed;
　– no discussion is allowed at this early stage; just put forward ideas.

◆ Keep these rules displayed as a continuous reminder.

◆ Brainstorm for 30 minutes or more and list *every* idea put forward (without judgment or discussion).

Follow this plan in selecting, evaluating, and implementing ideas.

◆ Divide participants into two subgroups and ask each group to place each idea into one of these categories:
A—important and feasible
B—possible
C—worthless

◆ Each group should put all **A** ideas on one sheet, **B** ideas on a second, and **C** ideas on a third sheet.

◆ Each person should examine both **A** lists and choose the two ideas that could make the greatest contribution. Each time an idea is chosen, check it off.

◆ Take the three ideas with the most check marks and ask each subgroup to choose the one idea that is the most important. Each group is then asked to prepare a written plan to implement the idea.

◆ After a specified time, perhaps six weeks, the whole group meets again to discuss how well plans are progressing and to agree on any necessary action.

◆ When the first ideas have been successfully implemented, the subgroups should be ready to move to other ideas. Project teams from outside the group can also be formed to help with implementing decisions.

SUMMARY

This chapter covered a lot of ground. We distinguished between handling complaints and managing them, and examined how to use complaints in a positive way to form a closer bond between your customers and yourself. The greatest benefit from complaints will be realized only if senior management shows its interest in resolving issues that have been identified and highlighted by the complaints.

This led to the subject of motivating your staff. We identified some of the major motivating factors, and we went on to examine practical ways of implementing activities that would support these factors.

Finally, we went into some detail of how to employ the brains and knowledge of your employees by discussing brainstorming and the need for proceeding in an organized fashion.

Chapter 6

Setting and Measuring Standards

The last chapter studied ways you can use complaints to help prove to customers that you genuinely want to satisfy their needs and how these same complaints can be used to stimulate your continuous improvement process throughout the company.

In order to prove to customers that you care about them, nothing can be left to chance. Your customer care program must be thoughtfully structured, accurately measured, and carefully managed. Therefore, this chapter explores:

◆ setting standards.

◆ measurements of results.

◆ feedback and use of data.

◆ management tools.

SETTING STANDARDS

It is important to agree to standards for as many activities as possible. These standards need not be set to provide the highest quality at any price—they should be set to meet or exceed customer-agreed or expected requirements. If no additional benefit is gained by you or the customer by setting an even higher standard, which may be expensive to achieve, then it would be wasteful to do so. However, if setting and conforming to a higher standard will give you a competitive advantage, you must carefully calculate the additional costs and balance these against the potential benefit.

If no standards are set, then each event will be determined by the prevailing attitude of the employee in question or the time that happens to be available. You cannot leave as important a factor as customer satisfaction to chance, and you must therefore set performance standards on individual tasks. It is similar to the process control approach in manufacturing, where you try to deviate from your standard within your limits as little as possible in order to give customers a uniform quality. In your case, the standards should be customer oriented and should be based on customer-expressed requirements. With the modern management tools available to you it is possible to measure achievements of many of these standards quite easily and, at the same time, to cater to customers' varied needs by agreeing on relevant standards for individual requirements.

In an endeavor to provide customers with the level of support they require, many companies now give the customers options as to which level is most appropriate to their specific operation. For instance, an example would be the laundry in a hotel, where the standard service may be for return within 24 hours but for an additional charge an express service is available for return within eight hours. Another example would be the service offered by overnight delivery services such as Federal Express, which offers the consumer a choice of two-day delivery, or next afternoon delivery for a higher price, or priority overnight delivery by the next morning for the highest price.

In support activities, customers can often choose a level of service or response and pay according to the level chosen. All these activities need standards to be set and conformance to these standards to be monitored. An ever-increasing number of organizations have developed "Customer Charters," which set standards for major factors important to the customer, and often these organizations accept penalty clauses that offer customers some compensation if the organization fails to perform to the set standards. In some cases customers require penalty clauses in their contracts to ensure that the promised support is delivered.

Examples of standards:

◆ time required to answer a telephone call

◆ time to respond to a letter or fax

◆ time required to resolve a problem

◆ frequency of management visits to customers

◆ anticipated time between breakdowns (MTBF = mean time between failures)

◆ mean time to repair (MTTR)

◆ frequency at which sites should be inspected for safety, cleanliness, or other relevant factors

◆ length of waiting lines

◆ response time to request for service

When you set these standards it is important to understand what effect conforming to these standards will have on customers and on your department, and you must ensure your ability to maintain the standards. Let us take the first standard in the list and examine it more closely.

It is not enough to set an average time for answering a telephone call; you must also specify the distribution of time around the average.

Distribution around an average

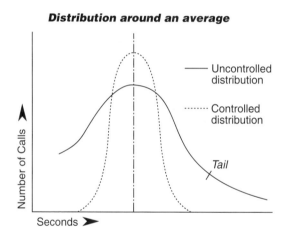

Let us assume that the average time to respond to a call is 10 seconds from the moment of the first ring. In an uncontrolled system this distribution is likely to have a number of calls replied to within three or four seconds and a "tail" of a small number of calls that may take 30 seconds to be answered. Individual customers are not really interested in your average. What they want to know is how long they have to wait. It is no use to point out to them that other customers (or even they themselves on another occasion) had their call answered promptly.

In consequence, your standard, in addition to giving the average, should also give a maximum time to ensure that a more normal distribution is achieved. By cutting off the tail you are going to get more satisfied customers because they are getting a more even service. In both cases the average is 10 seconds, but the standard deviation is different. You may know the story of the person having one foot in freezing water and the other in hot water—the average temperature may be a pleasant 35 degrees centigrade, but the person will be very uncomfortable.

The same approach applies to most of the standards mentioned. In some exceptional circumstances it may not be possible to meet the agreed-upon standards. In these, hopefully rare, instances it is essential to inform the customer prior to the occurrence or deadline that there will be a variance from the standard and a mutually acceptable solution will, in most cases, be found (see Chapter 4). Customers will be much less tolerant if the standard is not met without prior indication of this happening.

To summarize, standards should be:

◆ challenging but realistic.

◆ meaningful to customers and to your customer care vision.

◆ measurable wherever possible.

◆ regularly audited with necessary feedback.

MEASUREMENT OF RESULTS

Once you have agreed on standards, it is necessary to know how you are going to measure them, the frequency with which you will do so, and what you will do with the results.

Measuring against standards has been aided immensely by the use of modern management tools. In the past it would have been economically impossible to measure many of the activities now considered essential to satisfy customers. To use the same example as earlier in this chapter, measuring the time customers have to wait before a telephone call is answered and plotting distribution of telephone calls would have been difficult two or three decades ago, but now it can be done at a very reasonable cost. But just measuring what is happening is of little use unless you propose to do something positive to affect the situation.

Let us return to the telephone example. We will assume that your early measurements show that you have an uncontrolled condition with an unacceptably long tail as shown in the diagram. One way to resolve the situation would be to get more telephone operators and install more telephones lines, but this is likely to be an expensive solution. By studying the pattern of incoming calls, the source of calls, the distribution during the hours of the day and similar factors, more cost-effective solutions are feasible. It is usual in most businesses that the pattern of calls differs substantially between certain hours of the day, days of the week, or seasons of the year, enabling you to establish a clear trend. The source of calls may also show a bunching of customer and employee calls at the same period.

The job of a manager is, not surprisingly, to manage. To do that, managers need information. Once the information is on hand, it needs to be analyzed before ways of improving the situation are planned and action-oriented decisions taken. To continue with our example, the manager may decide to organize the company's own staff to make their calls at low activity periods (troughs on distribution graphs); flexible work hours may be introduced to give better coverage during peak periods; vacations or days off can be planned to avoid periods of peak activity; staff from other areas can be drafted at peak periods into relevant areas; or calls lasting a longer time can be transferred to other departments.

The essential points to bear in mind on measuring activities follow.

◆ What gets measured gets done.

◆ Results may be gradual—follow trends as well as absolute figures.

◆ Establish causes of variance (variance analysis).

◆ Data is only useful if it is utilized.

FEEDBACK

To obtain the basic data, you need feedback from customers as well as from your staff. Unless you demonstrate via senior management actions that you take the comments made by customers and staff seriously, the flow of information will dry up. Conversely, if you can show that you use the information to improve your customer care, the flow will continue.

Here are some ways companies encourage feedback.

◆ personalized letters

◆ management visits to customers

◆ short lines of communication, quick decisions, delegation

◆ customer help lines (careful monitoring of comments)

◆ customer surveys, questionnaires, audits

◆ staff training and development

◆ ideas workshop (caring approach but avoid wish lists)

◆ employee surveys

◆ involvement

◆ good database that is actively used

MANAGEMENT TOOLS

With the reduction in the cost of computer hardware, the availability of a wider range of software, and the advancement in telecommunication technology and its linking into computer technology for a multimedia approach, we now have much more efficient and cost-effective management tools available to improve customer care than we had just a few years ago.

The use of these tools must be carefully planned to ensure that they will help your staff to accomplish the required tasks most effectively, thus enabling you to give excellent customer care. At the same time, these tools should give you the management information you need to improve the efficiency of the operation. Many are available off the shelf as ready-to-use programs; others need to be adapted to specific needs or specially designed for individual purposes. Here we will mention only the most widely used aids to improve customer care.

Tracking pattern of telephone calls

This is used for many applications where the telephone is used extensively. It provides historical information on the number of calls received in each period of time, the time customers had to wait for the call to be answered, the length of the call, the number of calls abandoned before they were answered, and other relevant information. Many fax machines automatically print out similar information to enable fax usage to be monitored.

Response control centers

These are used by companies organizing outside activities of staff, such as on-site servicing of equipment and machinery, the tracking of police, ambulance, and fire staff and vehicles, and directing taxis to their destination, etc. These programs log each request, prioritize these calls within geographical areas, estimate the time of arrival, notify the appropriate person to carry out the requested activity, note the time of arrival, the time to perform the activity, and note the availability of the person or vehicle for further activities. They are linked to the company's database to enable information to be extracted as necessary to provide the relevant management information.

From this standard approach, more sophisticated programs have been developed for specific applications. For centers organizing the activities of service technicians, for instance, the system provides additional information to enable staff to forecast the workload for the next day or two and to indicate the likely cause of the problem. Thus they enable the technician with the appropriate skills, tools, and spare parts to be sent to the customer, to automatically replenish spare parts used by the technician during the visit, to initiate customer invoices, and from the subsequent feedback by the technician, to generate relevant reports. Where "smart" systems are used, the program then calculates any changes in probability since the initial identification of the problem.

In addition to the basic information enabling response times to be managed, other systems used, for example, by police departments, make it possible to locate individual vehicles and members of staff, and to record how long individual members have been on duty, and similar data.

Some companies also use their response time management systems as positive marketing and sales aids. Many invite key customers into their response centers to show them to what lengths the company has gone to handle customer calls efficiently. One taxi company provided a number of key customers with equipment (on loan) enabling these customers to enter the dispatch system direct (i.e., without having to talk to the taxi company's telephone operator). The initial purpose was only to reduce the taxi company's cost of having to answer the customer's telephone call and having to enter the information into the system. However, because the customer entered the system directly, it saved the operators time, the taxi arrived more quickly, and this attracted additional business from these customers to the taxi company. Thus, customer care was improved as well as profits.

Administrative aids

Computerized systems now enable regular customers to place their orders directly into the suppliers' systems, enabling them to establish current availability, prices, and other factors. The same entry is the basis for invoicing, which is initiated from the information provided by the shipping department. In the service industries, administrative systems enable banks and building societies to inform customers of their current account balance, to add interest to their accounts, and provide some tax information.

Many such systems were originally designed to reduce costs, but have since been developed further to improve customer support and generate additional business. Care must be taken not to depersonalize contact with the customer, as this might have a detrimental effect on customer relations. The skill of management is to find ways of utilizing management tools effectively to improve customer care, while also keeping in close contact with the customer.

SUMMARY

This chapter covered how to set standards and established that these standards must be customer oriented to give you the maximum benefit. To set market-oriented standards may necessitate subsidiary internal standards, which should, wherever possible, be specific, measurable, and must be monitored.

We examined various methods of measurement and how to use these measures. Feedback from customers and from your staff is essential and we looked at various ways of encouraging feedback.

Finally, there are a number of management tools that can be used to improve customer care. These management systems can be employed as sales and marketing aids to stimulate additional business and to demonstrate that the care of customers is important to your company.

Chapter 7

The Customer Care Program

In the last six chapters we have been examining individual aspects affecting customer care.

This chapter puts the individual items together into a total customer care program.

We will look at ways of:

◆ developing a coherent customer care program.

◆ selling this program inside the company.

◆ developing action plans.

◆ building on success.

DEVELOPING A CUSTOMER CARE PROGRAM

There are 13 steps in developing a customer care program.

1. Analyze current customer care requirements of the market.

2. Establish your company's position.

3. Specify your desired position.

4. Identify your options and the relevant resource requirements to move from your present position to the desired position.

5. Select options you will pursue.

6. Scrutinize "best practice" in customer care areas selected (benchmarking).

7. Appoint working parties to advance specific options selected.

8. Review results of working parties and develop a company-wide customer care plan.

9. Assign individual responsibilities for developing action plans and standards for each task.

10. Develop an implementation plan.

11. Implement the plan (fully or on a test basis).

12. Monitor initial results and adapt program as necessary.

13. Review at frequent intervals and provide feedback throughout the organization.

We will not examine each of these steps in detail, as most of them have already been discussed in previous chapters. However, there are just a few additional comments that may help you in developing a coherent customer care program.

◆ You must be brutally honest when examining your business and be realistic about its achievable progress.

◆ You must utilize all the company's knowledge and skills by involving as wide a range of staff as possible in developing and implementing your plans.

◆ You must prioritize your options not only by their financial benefits, but you should start by selecting projects for initial implementation that will give you positive results in a relatively short time, to encourage further activities.

◆ You must have a clear idea of what the desired aim of a project is and brief your staff accordingly.

◆ You must make sure that adequate manpower and financial resources are made available for progressing the customer care program, as well as for continuing your day-to-day activities efficiently in all units.

◆ You must keep your staff fully informed of progress at every stage of the program and particularly concentrate on how it has been received by customers. To use Tom Peters' dictum: *Celebrate success.*

INTERNAL SELLING

In most organizations there are people who overtly or covertly take a negative stance to any new program that naturally leads to change. Do not allow these attitudes to dampen the enthusiasm of other members of staff, but take suitable steps to discuss these matters with them privately. Specifically ask for their personal involvement, pointing out your need to utilize their skills and knowledge to further the aims of the company. Make them responsible for progressing certain activities that they can call their own, and make them feel an essential part of the team. Welcome any constructive criticism from them, but do not allow negative attitudes to infest the rest of your staff. Managers must learn to deal sympathetically but firmly with these individuals.

It is not only members of the staff that need to be persuaded that their personal involvement in developing and implementing customer care programs is necessary. Top executive management will also need to be persuaded that their personal commitment is essential and that platitudes will not be sufficient. It is often more difficult to show management in successful companies that change is necessary, as they often believe that what has worked in the past will also work in the future. Managers in successful companies should know that radical change is required. More recently all managers have come to realize that they must move with rapidly changing customer requirements and expectations.

How do you demonstrate to top management that their full commitment to customer support activities is essential? Top management have a large number of activities to coordinate and have to take decisions on many matters. They don't need any more problems! If you raise new issues with them, they want you also to present them with solutions.

Therefore, give them solutions.

◆ Quantify the profit impact of customer satisfaction.

◆ Identify the whole spectrum of support needed to satisfy customers.

◆ Present a proposed approach to reaching a solution.

◆ Indicate the likely financial and manpower resources required and a time frame.

The most difficult part of selling the need of this program to top management is to get a hearing. Here you need to use shock tactics by showing the reduction in profit currently caused by dissatisfied customers.

The next step is to demonstrate that you have given this matter considerable thought by presenting to them the approach outlined in the previous section.

Finally, obtain top management's full commitment to support the program and have a member of the top management team identified who will take personal responsibility for steering the program through every nook and cranny of the company.

You need to talk the language of senior management, a language they understand: *profit*. You should be able to demonstrate that lack of customer satisfaction is incurring additional costs to the company (dealing with complaints, making things right after they went wrong, finding new customers to replace those that moved away, and so on) and that it also decreases revenue through dissatisfied customers voting with their feet.

Top management will readily understand that satisfied customers are likely to provide you with more profit than dissatisfied ones. Often they do not appreciate that to satisfy customers more is required than a good product, a low price, and a strong sales force. This is the area where you must show that the loyalty of customers demands more than that; customers must be able to rely on the total support of their suppliers to work efficiently. You will have to convince all doubters that this requires a team effort. Therefore, the first-line management reader of this book is responsible for involving top management in a leadership role of the customer care effort.

BUILDING ON SUCCESS

Customer care does not have an immovable goal. The moment you reach your current targets, the goal posts change, and further improvements have to be made to keep up with a changing marketplace and more demanding customer expectations.

Build on your success, remotivate your team, recognize and reward achievements and encourage creativity.

Open communication with your customers and your staff should help you identify your joint achievements. It is up to you to use the methods discussed throughout this book to rekindle the fire of enthusiasm to discover additional ways of cementing your partnership relations with your customers. Like a rose garden, this relationship needs continual tending.

Do not rely on this happening on its own; you must actively promote continued improvements in this area. Customer care is an ongoing process that cannot be done once and just ticked off as completed.

SUMMARY

This book examined various aspects of customer care. Chapter 1 outlined customer care in general and its impact on company profits in particular, enumerating some of the main reasons for its growing importance in strategic and operational considerations. The first-line manager plays a key role in reorientating the company towards customer care.

Chapter 2 identified the need, not only for direct customer support, but also for support from staff further removed from customers; we introduced the concept of the internal customer. We went on to recognize the need for information on customer requirements and how to establish what these requirements are.

Chapter 3 explored the elements influencing customer care. We concentrated on skills and attitudes required by staff. Company procedures and systems have an important effect on your staff's ability to support customers efficiently. Finally, top management's approval, support, and leadership is vital.

Chapter 4 concentrated on enhancing customer relations and the need for creating a team approach throughout the company—the seamless organization. We then discussed communication skills with particular emphasis on active listening and telephone techniques.

Chapter 5 looked at complaints and how to use them as a positive influence on customer perceptions. It's important to separate the immediate need for *handling* complaints from the more long-term benefit obtained from *managing* complaints. We looked at ways of motivating staff and how to use brainstorming techniques.

Chapter 6 explained how to set standards for your various activities, how to measure them, and why you need to feed back information on results to your staff. We also examined a number of widely used management tools that facilitate customer support.

Finally in this chapter, we examined how to put together the various elements explained during the earlier parts of the book into a coherent customer care program, including action and implementation plans. We stressed the need for internal selling and reviewed a way of doing this within your organization.

Customer care is a never ending activity and you must therefore build on your past success to keep ahead of the game.

The thought I would like to leave with you is that everyone in the organization must be actively involved in customer care:

Customer care is not a spectator sport!

INDEX

BUSINESS ENGLISH

Second Edition • Andrea B. Geffner

DEVELOP EFFECTIVE BUSINESS WRITING SKILLS

BASIC RULES OF GRAMMAR AND USAGE
Subject and Verb • Sentence Structure • Punctuation • Abbreviation • Commonly Confused Words

MASTER EVERY CATEGORY OF BUSINESS CORRESPONDENCE
Memos • Letters • Reports • Models of each category show correct formats

NEW IN THIS EDITION
Advice for using electronic media • Guidelines for writing effective proposals

EXERCISES AND PRACTICE CORRESPONDENCE

BARRON'S

$12.95   Canada $16.95

Books may be purchased at your bookstore, or by mail from Barron's. Enclose check or money order for total amount plus sales tax where applicable and add 15% for postage and handling (minimum charge $4.95). Prices subject to change without notice. ISBN 0-8120-1441-3

Barron's Educational Series, Inc.
250 Wireless Boulevard, Hauppauge, NY 11788
In Canada: Georgetown Book Warehouse
34 Armstrong Avenue, Georgetown, Ont. L7G 4R9
(#31) R 10/96